FACULTY CLUB

University of California at Berkeley

BERNARD MAYBECK

JAMES STEELE

 ACADEMY EDITIONS

JAMES STEELE is an architect who has taught architecture at the University of Pennsylvania in Philadelphia, King Faisal University in Damman, Saudi Arabia and Texas Tech in Lubbock, Texas. He is currently Associate Professor at the University of Southern California, Los Angeles. He has also lectured at the Prince of Wales's Institute of Architecture in London. He is author of several books, including Academy Monograph No 13 *Hassan Fathy*, *Charles Rennie Mackintosh, Synthesis in Form* and *Museum Builders*.

ACKNOWLEDGEMENTS
I would like to thank Janet Lukehart and her staff at the University of California Faculty Club at Berkeley for all they have done to assist me in the preparation of this monograph, as well as Anthony Bliss at the Bancroft Library and Grier R Graff of Christopherson and Graff Architects in Berkeley for their co-operation in researching the archival photographs and working drawings of the original Maybeck building. All recent photographs, with the exception of those provided by Moore Ruble Yudell on pp33, 34 and one of the Great Hall by Richard Barnes/ Abbeville Press on pp52, 53, are graciously provided by Teresa Dahl. She was assisted by Kent McGrew and Elizabeth Monroe, who was also of enormous help to me. I would also like to thank Shereen Bar-Seif and Angelica Solis for preparing drawings for inclusion here, Carolyn Osborne for research and Sue Strakosch for preparation of the manuscript.
James Steele

Cover: Floor plan of Faculty Club at University of California at Berkeley, 1903. The Faculty Club was designed between 1902 and 1903 by Bernard Maybeck. It was subsequently added to in 1904, 1914, 1925 and 1956.

Historical Building Monograph No 5

First published in Great Britain in 1995 by
ACADEMY EDITIONS
An imprint of

ACADEMY GROUP LTD
42 Leinster Gardens, London W2 3AN
Member of the VCH Publishing Group

ISBN 1 85490 433 7

Distributed to the trade in the United States of America by
NATIONAL BOOK NETWORK, INC
4720 Boston Way, Lanham, Maryland 20706

Printed and bound in the United Kingdom

FACULTY CLUB

CONTENTS

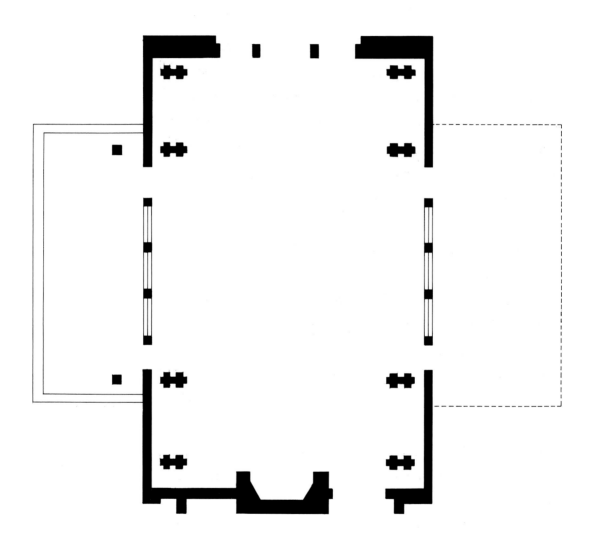

Maybeck's 1902 plan for the Faculty Club emphasises the importance of the Great Hall in future development

PREFACE

Bernard Maybeck's Faculty Club at Berkeley has for too long been the private memory of a relatively small number of enthusiasts. It is intended that this new critique will permit this important master-piece to be repositioned in history, for a wider international readership. In its handling of asymmetry with symmetry and volumetric massing the building established a unique harmony within the Great Hall, in the interaction of truss, arch, window, projecting cornice, trellis and gable.

There were important medieval and European resonances of an atavistic nature in this woodland setting when the building was complete, providing an important symbolic centring at the hearth for the staff of the rapidly expanding university in the early 1900s. At the same time Maybeck here prefigured important twentieth-century attitudes about image, and concerning functional determinism. There are valid comparisons here with the con-temporary works of Frank Lloyd Wright and the more recent architecture of San Francisco Bay Area, of Charles Moore's own Faculty Club for Santa Barbara, and indeed Moore's world famous Sea Ranch.

The Faculty Club at Berkeley by Bernard Maybeck is a work of significant influence today and important as a document in history to be more widely recognised.

Michael Spens

THE MAYBECK FACULTY CLUB
INSPIRATION AND CONTRADICTION

Born in Greenwich Village, New York City in 1862, Bernard Maybeck was the son of German *émigrés* who had arrived in America little more than a decade earlier. His father was a cabinet maker and Bernard became his apprentice, learning mechanical drawing, geometry and an appreciation of the rewards to be derived from a pain-staking attention to detail. Travel to France in 1881, on business related to his work with his father, brought him into contact with the Ecole des Beaux Arts. His subsequent interest in the school led to his entering and passing the difficult entrance examination in the following year. Lectures by Henry Lemmonier on Gothic architecture, the free classicism of his tutor Jules-Louis Andre, the legacy of structural determinism left by Viollet-le-Duc, and exhaustive surveys of French and German Romanesque and Gothic churches all had a lasting influence on Maybeck, and may be traced in varying degrees in all of the work that he later produced.

After arriving back in New York in 1884, Maybeck joined several other recent graduates from the Ecole in establishing an architectural practice, but his unpretentious emphasis on prag-matic craftsmanship, rather than on establishing the social connections necessary to thrive in Manhattan, prompted him to move west in 1889, to Kansas City, to seek a more substantial basis for his career. Friendships made there, in turn, encouraged him to move on to California and he travelled to San Francisco in November 1890.

San Francisco was in the midst of a building boom, a frontier city growing rapidly as a result of new railroad connections to the

Entrance to the Faculty Club

Midwest and the frenzy created by the gold rush. He and his wife settled in Oakland, and he found work with the Charles M Plum Company as a designer of custom made furniture and interiors, before an offer from A Page Brown made it possible for him to focus on architecture once again in the following year.

His subsequent involvement in the design of an entry for the World's Columbian Exposition in 1893 led to his being sent to Chicago to supervise construction of the 'California Building' that his firm had submitted. Its eclectic display of quasi-Spanish elements was similar to those used on the Ponce de Leon Hotel, in St Augustine, Florida, which he had worked on shortly after leaving the Ecole.[1] Like a surprising number of other influential architects of the time, such as Louis Sullivan, Adolf Loos and Frank Lloyd Wright, Maybeck was greatly impressed by the Columbia Exposition, which Daniel Burnham had intended to use as a platform from which to launch Classicism as the ideal civil and national style. Maybeck's Palace of Fine Arts, for the Panama–Pacific International Exposition that followed in San Francisco in 1913, shows the extent to which he was influenced by his brief stay in Chicago, and by the argument which Burnham had put forward, rather than by the exceptions to Classicism, such as the Ho-o-den Temple, which were sought out by Wright and Sullivan.

Maybeck moved to Berkeley shortly after returning from Chicago, to a neighbourhood close to the University of California, which in 1892 was surrounded by oak forests and green fields. His proximity to the University and the social contacts he made there, led to his appointment as a graphic arts instructor in 1894. This course developed over time, into a full architectural curriculum. He was also appointed Director of the Architectural Section of the Mark Hopkins Institute of Art in 1893, and these two initiatives, along with his increasing involvement in the University community, encouraged the architect,

View looking towards the entrance of the Faculty Club

Detail of the dragon head hammer-beams and columns in the Great Hall

who was then thirty-three years old, to begin private practice.

A remodelled one-storey cottage at Grove and Berryman Streets in Berkeley, which Maybeck extended in 1892, served as his studio, and shortly afterwards he received his first major commission, referred to him by the University President, Martin Kellogg. The client, Phoebe Hearst, wanted to erect a memorial to her late husband George Hearst, on the campus and responded enthusiastically to the preliminary scheme that Maybeck presented.

This meeting of Hearst and Maybeck was also instrumental in putting Maybeck in charge of administering and establishing a competition for a masterplan for the future growth of the University of California. A reception hall was also to be designed by Maybeck in which Mrs Hearst could participate in the formal ceremonies related to the competition.

Early in 1897 Maybeck travelled to Europe to enlist international entrants, especially at the Ecole des Beaux Arts, and to interview possible jurors, such as Norman Shaw, whom he and his wife visited in Hampstead.

There are intriguing similarities between Shaw's Holy Trinity Church on Latimer Road in West London, completed in 1886, and Maybeck's final design for what is now known as Hearst Hall. Primarily this is apparent in the form of the central vaulted nave, but rather than using steel girders to frame the steeply pitched painted arches of the Hall, as Shaw had done, Maybeck has used laminated wooden girders, making the angle of the sides steeper to avoid the cross ties seen in Holy Trinity Church.[2]

Possible parallels between these two buildings continue, as Maybeck also went on to visit Robert Sandilands, a classmate at the Ecole, in Glasgow, at the same time that Queen's Cross Church by Charles Rennie Mackintosh was being built. This has a nave that was also undoubtedly derived from Shaw's Holy Trinity Church.[3] Shaw appears

ABOVE and OPPOSITE: Wyntoon, residence of Pheobe Hearst, designed by Bernard Maybeck

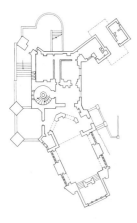

to have been Maybeck's main connection to the English Arts and Crafts Movement, but unlike its more progressive practitioners, such as Mackintosh, who sought a synthesis between industrial materials and craftsmanship in order to derive a contemporary architecture based in tradition, Maybeck adopted a reductive stance, similar to that of William Morris, best described in lectures such as 'Art and the Beauty of Life' delivered to the Birmingham Society of Arts in 1880, 'Gothic Architecture', printed by Kelmscott Press in 1893, and 'Art and Industry in the Fourteenth Century', in which Morris extolled the virtues of handicraft, particularly as practised in the Middle Ages.

Maybeck's medievalism is patently apparent in his second project for Phoebe Hearst, a residence which was executed after his return to California, called Wyntoon. This fanciful castle, rendered in lava rock, rubble stone and local timber with a green glazed tile roof, displays many of the same eccentricities that can be found in country houses of the same period, such as Cragside and Grim's Dyke, by Norman Shaw, and also has affinities with estates designed by H H Richardson in both massiveness of scale and in attempting to blend with rugged and natural surroundings.

In 1902, while working on Wyntoon, Maybeck learned that a committee, appointed by the officers of the Dining Association of the University, had recommended the formation of a faculty club and that the Board of Regents had offered a site in Strawberry Canyon, adjoining the Dining Association Building, for the project. Maybeck volunteered his services on March 10, 1902, according to a committee report, which also announced that $1,800 had been raised from the eighty members of the association, with $1,000 to become available through a ten year bond issue which would bear five per cent interest; and that the official name was to be The Faculty Club of the University of California.[4]

Ground floor plan of Wyntoon; OPPOSITE: Interior of the Great Hall, Faculty Club

Due to the limited budget, Maybeck proposed a single rectangular 'Great Hall' with a massive stone fireplace at its western end and French doors opening out on to open patios on each of its long sides. Flanking these windows are pairs of columns, terminating in extended capitals fancifully carved into dragons' heads, which support the steep wooden A-shaped trusses that form the main structure of the hall. Long purlins span horizontally between them as the secondary supports for the array of exposed roof rafters above.

The fireplace, as the focal point of the room, held a similar symbolic meaning for Maybeck as it did in the early work of Frank Lloyd Wright, before the collapse of domestic tranquillity in Oak Park caused the latter to re-evaluate the significance and position of the hearth. In this instance, Maybeck used the fireplace as a symbol of the collegial spirit, by evoking the most basic human instincts of unity around a fire. The ingenuity of his fireplace design has assumed almost legendary status among his clients and their descendants, who have uniformly praised his ability to calculate the critical relationships between width, throat and draught. His unerring instincts in balancing these dimensions, which defy tabular statistical selection, have ensured that even his largest fireplaces, such as the massive baronial example in the Roos House, do not direct smoke into the room instead of up the chimney.

Later in his life, Maybeck would sketch the Kern house in Yorkville on Manhattan Island, a place he had frequently visited as a child and where his mother had been raised. His ability to graphically reproduce the house from memory indicates that it had a deep impression on him. In proportion, the plan is similar to the Great Hall of the Faculty Club, a rectangular volume with extended, open porches on each of its long sides; a typology the architect obviously associated with the idea of home. Taken together, the large projecting manorial fireplace, the paired trusses and columns with dragon

Great Hall, Faculty Club, looking towards Maybeck's fireplace

head hammer-beams, the exposed purlins and rafters, and the steeply pitched roof all in wood, give this original section of the Faculty Club the dark primal aspect of the hall described in the epic *Beowulf*, with natural light only introduced in the centre of the long walls. The record of the first meeting of the club, held on September 16, 1902 indicates that the most memorable part of the ceremony was the lighting of the inaugural fire on the large hearth stone. Maybeck had accurately gauged the symbolic significance that this basic element would play in the institution, and his assessment has proven to be correct.

Construction, under the architect's supervision, was already under way when several members suggested the possibility of a residential wing, with rooms to be financed by those who wanted them. A contract, signed on June 20, during construction of the Great Hall, indicates that four members arranged to supply materials and labour needed for living quarters, with the provision that they could occupy them rent-free for ten years. A preliminary plan by Maybeck shows that the extension to accommodate these was originally drawn on the first elevation of the Great Hall. Presumably the arrangements with the individuals involved could not be finalised in time to build both parts together, making it necessary to treat the rooms as a second phase.[5] The extension to include these rooms, which is slightly narrower than the Great Hall, extends out horizontally to the west, and is slightly less than twice as long as the original Club. The juncture between the first and second phase was used by the architect as an opportunity to include a main entrance, and staircase up to the rooms above, emphasised by a tower, which was the suite of one of the four residents. The lower level also had a fireplace, a billiard room and an office.

At this point, Maybeck's involvement in both the design and construction of the Faculty Club was complete. What he managed to achieve, in spite of the incongruity of the programme given to him, was a unified expression of the structural function, with one notable exception. The roof line of the original club, as well as the extension that followed it, bears no relation to the steeply pitched trusses of the Great Hall; a direct contradiction of the principle of honest external structural expression rigorously emphasised by Jules-Louis Andre, his tutor at the Ecole des Beaux Arts. This is especially uncharacteristic, given the profiles of two other club-houses that bracket this project, namely the Town and Gown Clubhouse at Berkeley of 1899, which has carefully designed roof extensions, and the Outdoor Art Clubhouse in Mill Valley in 1905, with its beams that puncture the high roof to reach columns out-side. One can only speculate on the reasons for this aberration. The Panama–Pacific International Exposition, which began the trend towards the Spanish Mission Style, was still more than a decade away. There were stirrings towards this direction however, in the work of other architects soon after the turn of the century in Berkeley, in the design of St Mark's Episcopal Church and the Santa Fe Railroad Station. The former has been traced to additional designs provided for the Pan–American Exposition held in Buffalo, New York in 1900, and was more specifically patterned after the Mission San Carlos Borromeo in Carmel, and the San Luis Rey Mission. The latter mission has also been identified as the source of a specific roof profile called an *espadana*, made up of juxtaposed curvilinear and orthogonal forms. In a description of this mission, it has been noted:

> . . . these elevated curved gables were somehow believed to be a further protection against earthquake damage. The Espadana facade was thought to have come from the corbie gables of Belgium, Holland and Germany, since some seventeenth-century Spanish colonial architects were from these countries.[6]

Faculty Club, circa 1903, prior to extensions by John Galen Howard

Faculty Club, after the addition to the north elevation

Eastern elevation of the Faculty Club

His possible familiarity with the corbie or crow step gable aside, Maybeck's only concession to the Mission influence on the exterior of the Faculty Club is in his use of a shallow pitched tile roof, stucco walls, arches over major openings, and exposed wooden rafters, left plain in most cases, but ornately carved in the pergola over the external porch of the Great Hall. On such a plain, linear expanse of white wall, ornamental relief takes on heightened visual significance, and Maybeck understood the impact that small details would have on such a surface, especially when repeated. A projecting band of casement windows related to the residential rooms on the north elevation, as well as an exposed truss on the gable end of the tower provide such relief, making the walls seem even more substantial by contrast, and 'grounding' the building, as Ester McCoy has observed in her classic study of early Californian architecture.[7]

The Maybeck assembly of 1900 is also a masterpiece of variance within a similar tectonic language; asymmetrical symmetry in volumetric massing. The counterpoint created by the foursquare Great Hall, with its projecting porch and trellis, the soaring central tower which acts as a solid vertical fulcrum, and the directional thrust of the second, residential component which extends out along a slightly lower horizontal line from it, is perfectly balanced but difficult to assess quantitatively. Each element of truss, arch, window, projecting cornice, trellis or gable interacts so intricately with all of the other exceptions to the solid plaster wall that any further variation, however slight, disrupts the delicate harmony of the entire composition. The first of several expansions designed by John Galen Howard which followed, shows the fragility of that balance. His addition to the Maybeck scheme in 1904 makes best use of the linearity of the existing building, and avoids the highly visible north facade in favour of the less semiotically charged elevation on the south.

This move by Howard was pragmatically as well as symbolically sound and is surprisingly sensitive, considering the fact that he was Maybeck's nemesis, and held his predecessor in extremely low regard. McCoy has related that:

> According to William Gray Purcell, who had worked . . . as a draftsman in Howard's office, Howard considered Maybeck's work beneath serious consideration. Maybeck's name was greeted with laughter in the drafting room. Soon after Howard moved to California in 1901, he was appointed Professor of Architecture; and Maybeck was suddenly out of a post at the university.[8]

Howard's own house, at 2421 Ridge Road, designed shortly after his arrival in Berkeley, and his Hearst Mining Hall, a commission taken away from Maybeck, partially reveal the basis for this disparity: in particular, Howard's emphasis on non-telluric materials which

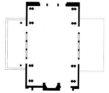
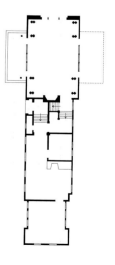

Sequence of plan development from 1902-14

Maybeck did not use until much later in his career. The ground
floor of Howard's extension to Maybeck's original Faculty Club
ensemble, technically the third phase of the complex, was intended
to accommodate the billiard room, which was relocated due to the
expanding social function of the Club, as well as a secretary's office
and servants' quarters.[9] The first floor of the addition is basically
square in plan, projecting out at a right angle from the southern
porch of the first Great Hall and makes an 'L' of Maybeck's strictly
linear scheme. It provided additional residential quarters, including
bedrooms and studies for two more faculty members with a second
stairway appended to Maybeck's central set to allow private access
to them. A porch, intended to replace the outdoor room on the
southern elevation subsumed by the addition, ran along the entire
western exposure of Howard's portion, ideally positioned to take
advantage of late afternoon sun. Following the precedent set by

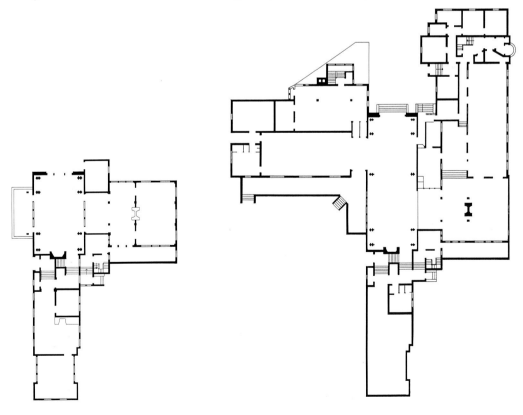

earlier residents, this addition was paid for by the two professors housed there, in return for free accommodation for ten years. Two years later, as a club historian has recorded:

> The Directors opened a subscription for bonds in the amount of $13,000 and the entire issue was immediately subscribed or guaranteed. The funds raised were used to absorb the old University Dining Association, to buy out the rent-free contracts of those professors who had built the western and southern additions, and to clear all the other indebtedness to the Club.[10]

Relaxation of the qualification for membership to include associate status which allowed prominent community leaders to join the Faculty Club, as well as the increasing scope of its activities, made further expansion inevitable. Subsequent additions were carried out in 1914, nearly doubling the membership to 575, while others in 1925 and 1956 further obscured Maybeck's original core.

Southern elevation of the Faculty Club

The Berkeley Faculty Club has an important historical position as a transitional work, feeding contemporary pluralism by prefiguring certain attitudes about image and the exclusive iconography of functional determinism. Recognition of this has generally been confined to a group of local admirers, but the precise ways in which this single example of Maybeck's *œuvre* have actually contributed to the current dialectic have yet to be specified categorically.

To begin to do so, it is necessary to stress that this commission was completed relatively early in Maybeck's career, eighteen years after leaving the Ecole des Beaux Arts, little more than a decade after arriving in San Francisco from the Midwest, and eight years before designing the First Church of Christ Scientist, which is his masterpiece. His chronology of work, ending seventeen years before his death in 1957, is prodigious; his durability of incalculable significance in helping to establish his international reputation. His dates of birth and death are close to those of Frank Lloyd Wright, with whom he has frequently been compared, but aside from extent, their careers were completely different and attempts to establish other parallels are typically forced and unconvincing. Indisputable similarities include their early devotion to the Arts and Crafts ideal of the total work of art, and their fascination with the formal potential of wood, especially reinforced in Wright's design of his Oak Park Studio and House.

After his deliberate divorce from the domestic security of Oak Park however, Wright relentlessly sought a solution to the central issue that had been eluding Arts and Crafts theorists such as Ruskin and Morris, and which was only really addressed by Mackintosh, in the circle of his Glasgow School of Art, and which was characterised as the marriage of tradition and the machine. In the Barnsdall House, which was Wright's first commission after making the same pilgrimage as Maybeck, from the heartland of America to its final frontier in California, he made a determined effort to disguise the wooden frame of the house, wrapping it in stucco to resemble concrete. Although Wright was searching for a new, truly American successor to the Prairie Style he left behind in Illinois, the approach that he adopted for Barnsdall was quasi-Mayan and there are intriguing comparisons to be made with Maybeck's Faculty Club which was externally patterned after a Spanish Mission. Both buildings represent anomalies in the languages evolved by their respective architects, and they each looked south for a new interpretation. The extent of the variance is critical, since both consistently reiterated their belief in the honesty of structural and material expression, as well as the formal delineation of function. Wright, however, used the theoretical and psychological hiatus offered by the Barnsdall commission as an opportunity to explore a new direction, which emerged as the concrete or textile block houses in Los Angeles in the late 1920s. These were described by Wright in his *Autobiography* as his attempt to finally come to grips with the 'machine', even if the machine in this instance was a muscular construction worker who was the only person able to press the blocks from a single metal mould. Falling into the familiar trap traceable in other contemporary designs such as Le Corbusier's Salvation Army Headquarters in Paris, of having to custom-fabricate certain elements to make the entire building appear to be standardised, Wright nonetheless felt that he was finally participating in the Industrial Age. While the hand production of these textile blocks still places them in the Crafts tradition, they made the architect's next leap to the Johnson Wax Headquarters and Fallingwater, and eventually to the Guggenheim Museum, a philosophical probability. The Faculty Club, on the other hand, really is the exception that proves the rule, with the buildings that followed reverting to the pattern set in Maybeck's previous work. The Kellogg House, built in the month following the architect's last stage of the Faculty Club, as well as the Stockton, Boke, Dresslar and Keeler houses completed before Wyntoon in 1903, all signal a return to the architect's penchant for a clear volumetric expression, painstakingly hand-crafted in wood.

It took the earthquake and subsequent fire which devastated San Francisco on April 18, 1906 to alter Maybeck's commitment to wood. The concrete Lawson House that followed, in 1907, was a direct result of the owner's desire for a more secure shelter. Kenneth Cardwell, who has been one of the first to systematically catalogue Maybeck's work, has explained that this initial instance of the architect's conversion from Gothic Medievalism to Classicism, along with the Oscar Maurer Studio of the same year, stemmed from the 'historical connection that Maybeck made between the destruction of San Francisco and Pompeii. He would design as would a Pompeiian architect, but with modern materials and methods.'[11]

Detail of the ceiling structure of the Great Hall, Faculty Club

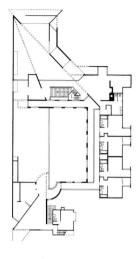

His epiphany was short-lived however, and this initial foray into an industrial medium, which could only be rationalised through romantic associations, was soon abandoned for a more familiar style. This was soon followed by the residential architecture that has come to most represent Maybeck in the public consciousness. The Albert Schneider, Leon Roos, Samuel Goslinsky and the architect's own, second house, tragically and ironically destroyed by fire in 1923, were all completed between the San Francisco earthquake and the construction of the First Church of Christ Scientist. These have come to define Bay Region architecture at its zenith, the prototypical combination of prominent, wide-eaved roof, well-ordered rectilinear plan, and wooden frame, frequently utilising a redwood shake skin, persisting through the translations of William Wurster in the mid to late 1960s.

Charles Moore also considered himself a part of the Bay Region tradition and his work in the early 60s around Berkeley indicates an empathy with this profile. While the Sea Ranch, a recognised marker of the change of spirit in architecture in 1966, continues this language, his Faculty Club at the University of California at Santa Barbara, built two years later, refracts it, becoming even more instrumental in the fragmentation that followed. The model for this later rendition was its namesake in Berkeley, the anomaly which proved to be more fascinating to Moore's complex and lively imagination than the typology Maybeck evolved soon afterwards. Like Maybeck, Moore was also faced with a restricted budget, but labour and material costs had risen dramatically in the sixty-four years that separate the two buildings, forcing him to use less massive walls, and no visible wood at all. Once that obvious difference is taken into account, it is possible to see that it is the discrepancy between the envelope and the angular interior exoskeleton of the Berkeley club that intrigued Moore rather than the more formalistic efforts

The Faculty Club at Santa Barbara, 1968, by Charles Moore, plan (above) and exterior view (opposite)

Faculty Club at Santa Barbara, 1968, by Charles Moore

that bracket it, and it was the unseen gap between sharp wooden trusses and the actual flat angles of the Mission Style roof which piqued his boundless curiosity. In describing his intention for the First Church of Christ Scientist, Maybeck had said that he wanted it to be 'the same on the inside as the outside, without sham or hypocrisy', while the dichotomy of the most major precedents was possibly not even evident to him.[12]

On the interior of the Santa Barbara Faculty Club, Moore has repeatedly pierced the walls of the soaring dining area to show the outer envelope beyond, literally adding a new spatial dimension to this historical reference. There are familiar quotes everywhere, altered just enough to qualify as commentary instead of translation; the structuralist foray into the deeper meanings of language just beginning to be applied to architecture in experimental ways. Those quotes extend to the John Galen Howard addition to the linear assembly that Maybeck had produced, unquestionably the most sensitive of all those that were to follow in spite of the enmity between the two rival architects. To articulate his extension, which is on a perpendicular axis to the original Great Hall, Howard used an angular skylight as a translucent parenthesis between the two. The device is simple but surprisingly effective, allowing a view of the exterior of the older section from the entrance to Howard's newer section. It is utilised again as a continuous device for allowing light around the perimeter of the central courtyard in Moore's Faculty Club at Santa Barbara. This courtyard, as an enlarged version of one of the favourite spaces of the Berkeley original, continues the comparison, but the list of similarities between the two buildings extends from Moore's playful translation of the leaded glass banners surrounding the Great Hall into neon tubes, down to the most minute detail.

By ripping away pieces of the Gothic interior that Maybeck had inserted into the Mission Style shell, and by abstracting the idea of the interchangeability of viscera and sheath, Charles Moore at Santa Barbara intentionally opened up a new front in the offensive on the curtain wall. The Santa Barbara Faculty Club was initially published in a particularly influential issue of *Perspecta*, along with Moore's article 'You Have to Pay for the Public Life', which was released at the same time as Robert Venturi's *Complexity and Contradiction in Architecture*. Venturi's use of layering, first seen in the Nurse's Association Building in Ambler, and also his mother's house in Chestnut Hill, was ostensibly prompted by Louis Kahn, who had used it in the Luanda Embassy as a device for environmental control. Although the debate about who was most influenced by who still continues, Venturi's transformation of Kahn's attempt to 'wrap ruins around buildings', had more to do with subliminal inference than sensorial control, the semiotics of 'inscription' as Peter Eisenman has called the syntactical use of the various elements of a building. Kahn's glare-reducing second skin, converted to a device by which to signal symbolic content and exaggerate ironic references by Robert Venturi, takes on a different purpose in Charles Moore's hands, as an explication of regional tradition, or the diachronic essence at its source.

As one of the primary subjects of that inquiry, Maybeck was the antithesis of the modern adventurer, his legendary creativity a symptom of cultural continuity rather than individual speculation. Once again speaking of his design for the First Church of Christ Scientist, he offered an insight into this aspect of his character when he said, as Cardwell relates:

> ... he felt that he had been hired by a group of people as sincere as he believed people were in the eleventh and twelfth centuries. He therefore tried to imagine himself as a twelfth-century designer, imbued with this same sincerity.[13]

As a displaced medievalist seemingly caught in a time warp, Maybeck worked slowly and methodically to create a community of his own making in Berkeley, building after building incrementally contributing to a unified vision of what he thought a village should be. That sense of displacement, however, manifested itself in his eclecticism, and nowhere more emphatically than in the disjuncture evident between the internal and external expressions of the Faculty Club. Anthony Giddens has described the dilemma well in saying that:

> In traditional culture, the past is honoured and symbols are valued because they contain and perpetuate the experience of generations. Tradition is a mode of integrating the reflexive monitoring of action with the time-space organisation of the community . . . Tradition is not wholly static, because it has to be reinvented by each new generation as it takes over its cultural inheritance from those preceding it.

In the modern condition, however, as he goes on to explain:

> . . . reflexivity takes on a different character. It is introduced into the very basis of system reproduction, such that thought and action are constantly refracted back upon one another . . . To sanction a practice because it is traditional will not do; tradition can be justified, but only in the light of knowledge which is not itself authenticated by tradition.[14]

The recurring symbols that Maybeck has used, such as his swirling adaptation of Gothic tracery, and carved wooden beam ends, found as a continuous refrain, testify to his instinct for perpetuation; while the laminated arches of Hearst Hall in 1899, and the Boys Club for the San Francisco Settlement Association in 1910, as well as his later use of pre-cast concrete in the Wallen W Maybeck house in Contra Costa County in 1937, clearly demonstrate his unequalled capacity for re-invention. He is the embodiment of the dilemma created by modernity that made it impossible to return to a purely vernacular expression; the idea that Adolf Loos attempted to convey in his own writing and architecture.

Of all of the transitional architects who found inspiration in his work, only Charles Moore seemed to comprehend the fracture that Maybeck personified, best expressed in the vale of the University of California at Berkeley, beside Strawberry Creek. Moore's own rendition was as seminal, in its own way, as the Vanna Venturi House, which was seized upon by a generation of young architects who, unaware of the source, responded to the novelty of its form, rather than its content. This influence was most profound in Moore's own subsequent work, which has been preliminarily catalogued but has yet to be placed into historical perspective following his death in 1994. There is a marked similarity between many of the plans Moore produced after the Faculty Club at Santa Barbara and Maybeck at his best; Moore's Tempchin, Koizim, Saz and Burns House, completed between 1969 and 1974, exhibit the most obvious parallels in their volumetric verticality, spatial interrelationships and openness, structural originality and inventiveness and overall configuration.

While Maybeck based his most stylistically diverse work on the obvious juncture between the Old and New Worlds, in an attempt to reconcile them, the Gothic and Mission styles underline the fault which Charles Moore instinctively identified. As one critic has noted:

> The architecture of Spanish California – the missions, their outlying buildings, the adobe dwellings – had special appeal because it represented a valid local past worth exploring and satisfied yearnings to find some old roots in a new land.[15]

While valid, that past was also troubled, and not nearly as romantic and utopian as those followers who had idealised Maybeck's initial interpretations had led the public to believe.

Towards the end of the eighteenth century, Franciscan missionaries, led by Juanipero Serra, embarked on what can only be characterised as a colonial enterprise. Acting with the full authority of the Spanish government, they initially intended that they would occupy and hold 'in trust' the lands of the native Americans, while they educated their inhabitants and brought them into the Catholic fold. To do this, they established more than twenty fortresses for the Church, from San Juan Capistrano below Los Angeles to the south, to San Juan Bautista near San Francisco to the north, all built between 1769 and 1823. They were conceived as self-sufficient compounds, each supplied with a garrison of soldiers to ensure that the conversion process went smoothly, and in case it did not, each was located one day's journey from the next, along the Camino Real, or Royal Road. In addition to the requisite church, each mission contained workshops, primarily intended for weaving fabric for clothes, a huge kitchen and refectory, living quarters, stables and cattle pens, all typically organised around one or more large central courtyards. The compounds were built with mud bricks covered in plaster, with the church bell and other minimal iron work being the only materials not readily available on site. Colour was added to the plaster covering to individualise each mission; for example, San Carlos Borromeo near Carmel was trimmed in pale yellow, to offset the walls, which are in this instance made from sandstone quarried nearby, while pastel shades from both ends of the colour spectrum were utilised elsewhere.

By the time California transferred from Spanish to Mexican control in 1821, and the missions converted to haciendas under individual governors or families, nearly one-third of the native American population that the Spanish had intended to save had been decimated by various imported diseases, and their subsequent fate

Detail of porch pergola adjacent to entrance, showing hammer-beams piercing the external wall of the Great Hall, Faculty Club

under governmental changes that followed was even worse.

Although badly damaged by an earthquake in 1812, San Juan Capistrano, which is perhaps the best known of the missions because of the swallows that return to it each year, still has the adobe chapel which Juanipero Serra built there in 1776, now marked by a large statue of Serra blessing an inhabitant of the mission. At the height of its activity under the Franciscans, nearly a thousand of those made wards of the Church by the Spanish government would come in from the fields surrounding the mission to eat in its series of arcaded courtyards, and it produced five hundred thousand pounds of wheat, more than two hundred thousand pounds of corn, and fourteen thousand head of cattle annually. A large gristmill ground the corn and wheat into flour for tortillas and bread, baked in two large ovens, and a tannery processed cowhides for various uses.

Seeing San Juan Capistrano today, it is easy to understand how the architectural product of the Mission system was appreciated, and rationalised as something separate from the system itself. A system which is now being equated by many historians as an organised programme of exploitation and genocide, regardless of its lofty ideals. Although later used by less sensitive architects than Maybeck to promote an image of California that would lure eager immigrants from the east and Midwestern United States and feed the excessive land speculation taking place in the early part of the twentieth century, the Mission Style, in his hands, was understated and noble. He was especially attuned to the aspect of colour, and his selections, as described by those who saw them when they were first applied, were audacious without being gauche, balancing the heaviness of the plaster walls. He is known to have covered several walls in citrine-coloured burlap alternately attached with thin wooden strips stained dark brown. Rather than paint the

Approach to the Faculty Club

exterior of the building however, he took a more subtle approach.
As Ester McCoy explains:

> The Faculty Club was one of Maybeck's first experiments
> with texture in plaster. He disliked the raw newness of plas-
> ter and tried to capture the texture of the adobe and straw
> walls of the missions. In 1900 stucco was considered a cheap
> imitation of stone, just as shingles were considered proper
> only for the simple house. Maybeck made them both a part
> of his vocabulary in architecture.[16]

The complete story regarding Maybeck's use of colour is more
complicated than this would imply, extending to his attitude towards nature and his attempts to relate buildings to their sites in
subtle, effective ways through the use of specific planting. In his
study of Maybeck's work, Kenneth Cardwell has mentioned that
Maybeck's awareness of the potential of landscaping increased
dramatically about ten years after his arrival in Berkeley, prompted
by the interest that his wife Annie began to show in the subject.
The Faculty Club marks the beginning of this phase; the site itself
providing the impetus for the architectural response rather than
the reverse. The location of the original dining hall, which Maybeck
was asked to extend, dictated the starting point, but there were
several other options that he could have chosen, given the expanse
of the area provided. He decided to extend the building in a straight
line, parallel to a high ridge to the south and to the north, a deep,
torrential stream called, deceptively, Strawberry Creek. Thus he
delineated territory in much the same way that Italian Rationalist
architects, such as Mario Botta, do today. Maybeck, however, read
the spectacular site he had been given and responded with a building that is both insular and directly connected to its surroundings.
Ancient oak trees, individual to the site, were treated reverentially
by the architect, and were obviously considered in the composition

Porch on the northern side of the Great Hall, Faculty Club

of his main entrance elevation. The single arched window on this facade, which is painted the same forest green as the other double-hung frames next to it, is positioned on axis with the most sculptural oak tree, a twisted gnarled specimen which becomes an extramural part of the architecture.

In addition there are numerous instances of attempts to join the natural and artificial – most notably in Maybeck's pergola-terraces, physical gestures projecting into the green perimeter – to the extent that the structure of these porch coverings is a continuation of the hammer-beams that support the inner hall. While those who look for evidence of contradiction and dislocation make much of the intentional division between the stylistic language of the internal and external skins, there is also a less discernible but equally potent statement of the architect's intent of linking the inside and outside realms by means of the lateral structure piercing the external wall to become the beams of the porch or pergola beyond.

This device of stylistic duplicity, exposed by structural excision and continuity is not found elsewhere in Maybeck's work, although he may be seen later on to be fond of similar piercings in the cause of structural honesty. The implication here is that the primal power of the site, which is a microcosm of Edenic images complete with forest, mountain, river and field, prompted Maybeck to respond in a more forceful way than he would have otherwise, and to protect the fragile Gothic forms that he preferred inside a more linear solid than he would use elsewhere. This aspect, of creating a building in deference to a pre-existing condition, rather than combining the two as he would later, is important to understanding the significance of the Berkeley Faculty Club and its place in the architect's work.

Soon afterwards, Maybeck began supplying the same natural context that he had been provided with at the University, on more mundane and less magnificently bucolic properties than he had

Window detail of the Faculty Club

worked on there. To those few who have seen his original drawings he is acknowledged as an accomplished landscape architect.
These rough studies illustrate how keen he was to formulate a
connection between his architecture and nature. As one has described them, after seeing studies for the unrealised project of
another Church of Christ Scientist in San Francisco:

> These church drawings are unlike most other architectural
> drawings in several ways. Rendered in brilliant, flat gouache
> on brown kraft paper, the drawings are bursting with land-
> scape. Planting is everywhere in these renderings, often cov-
> ering the very buildings the architect was seeking to pro-
> mote. Second, this planting is not the generic, blurry sort of
> 'shrubbing up' one sees as entourage, surrounding most ar-
> chitects' elaborately detailed buildings. This was planting de-
> sign carefully composed with detailed and identifiable indi-
> vidual shrubs, trees, flowers and vines. Third, in each of the
> church interior sections and elevations, Maybeck had care-
> fully delineated the vegetation that would be viewed behind
> his trademark industrial sash windows, making clear his in-
> tent that the planting behind them was to be used as part of
> the 'buildings' ornament'.[17]

In addition to colouring parts of the exterior of his buildings in
response to landscape groupings nearby, and positioning and sizing
window openings to provide a better view of them, as he did at the
Berkeley Faculty Club, in his later work he also chose plants as
vignettes to be seen in framed view and also to project their colours
into various rooms. Wisteria was one of his favourite choices, trained
on to pergolas over porches, as in the Faculty Club and First Church
of Christ Scientist, and it eventually grew to cover a substantial part
of the exterior elevation of the former, blurring the delineation
between nature and the built artefact, as it was meant to do.

Maybeck's interest in landscape design is felt to have come from Jules-Louis Andre who was one of his instructors at the Ecole des Beaux Arts; the same man who encouraged the refinement of the idea of *caractére*, or honesty of internal structural expression on the exterior of a building. Maybeck saw, and wrote about California as 'a garden spot on earth' and frequently made comparisons between its climate and that of the Mediterranean. Along with his wife, he was one of the founding members of the Hillside Club in 1898, which sponsored environmental awareness and protective action to protect Berkeley from the dangers of rapid growth.

The enduring value of the Faculty Club is demonstrated by its role in inspiring new forms and its ability to be added to over time by many others without changing its overall concept. It remains a viable example of pluralistic authority for us today.

NOTES

1 Kenneth H Cardwell, *Bernard Maybeck: Artisan, Architect, Artist*, Peregrine Smith (Santa Barbara, California) 1977, p31.

2 Andrew Saint, *Richard Norman Shaw*, Yale University Press (New York) 1976, p288-9.

3 James Steele, *Charles Rennie Mackintosh: Synthesis in Form*, Academy Editions (London) 1994, p36-7.

4 James Gilbert Paltridge, *A History of the Faculty Club at Berkeley*, The Faculty Club, University of California (Berkeley, California) 1990, p9.

5 Robert Bernhardi, *The Buildings of Berkeley*, Holmes Book Company (Oakland, California) 1972, p32. *Stanford University*, 1891, is another source.

6 Ibid, p53.

7 Ester McCoy, *Five California Architects*, Reinhold (New York) 1960, p13.

8 Ibid, p25.

9 Paltridge, op cit, p16.

10 Paltridge, op cit, p16.

11 Cardwell, op cit, p98.

12 Ibid, p122.

13 Cardwell, op cit, p26.

14 Anthony Giddens, *The Consequences of Modernity*, Stanford University Press (California) 1990

15 Bernhardi, op cit, p18.

16 McCoy, op cit.

17 Catherine Howett, 'Frank Lloyd Wright and American Residential Landscaping', *Landscape*, no 26, 1982, p64.

Interior of the Great Hall

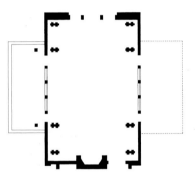

Maybeck's original 1902 plan for the Great Hall

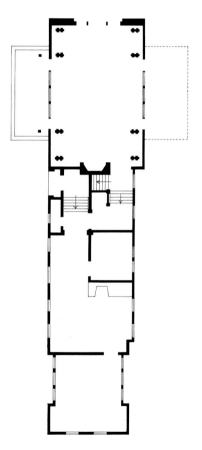

Maybeck's design of 1903 incorporating the residential wing; OVERLEAF: Present day approach to the Faculty Club

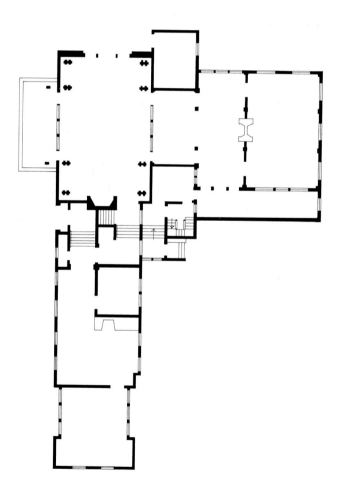

Faculty Club plan after initial extension in 1904 by John Galen Howard

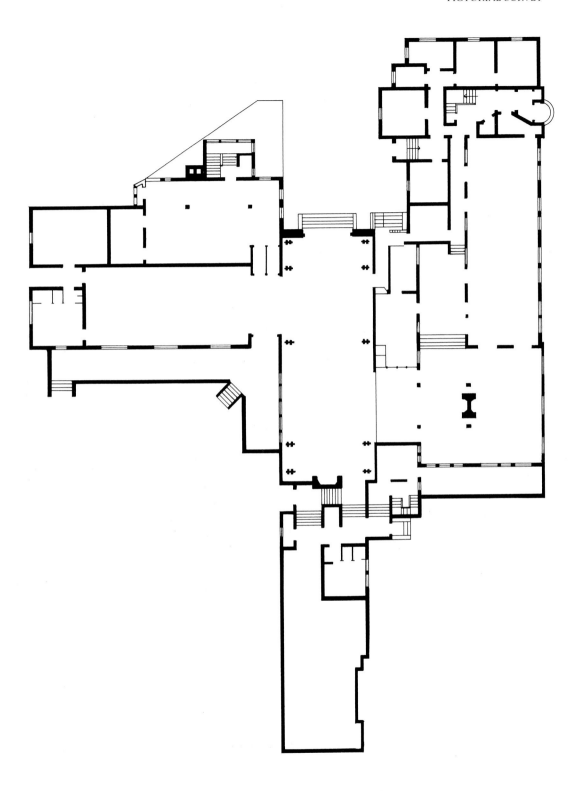

Plan of the Faculty Club in 1914; OVERLEAF: Interior of Great Hall

Roof plan after the additions of 1956

Roof terrace of the Faculty Club

Interior of Great Hall

Glazed screen to Great Hall

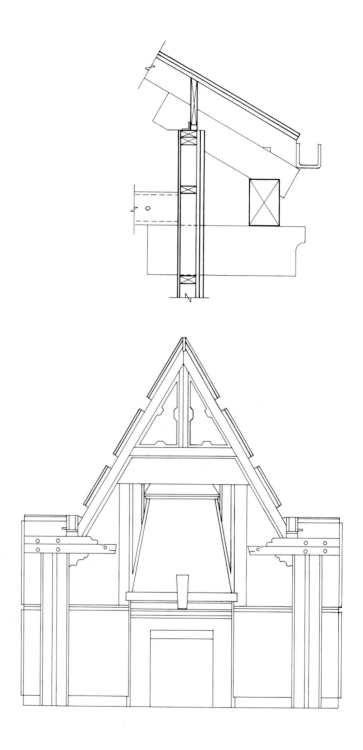

FROM ABOVE: Eaves detail; section through the Great Hall

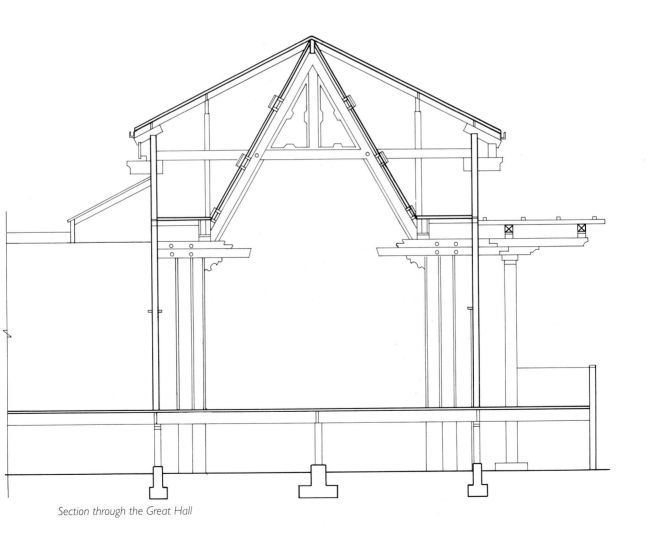

Section through the Great Hall

OPPOSITE: Glazed skylight between the Maybeck and Howard sections; FROM ABOVE: Arched window detail; Fireplace by John Galen Howard

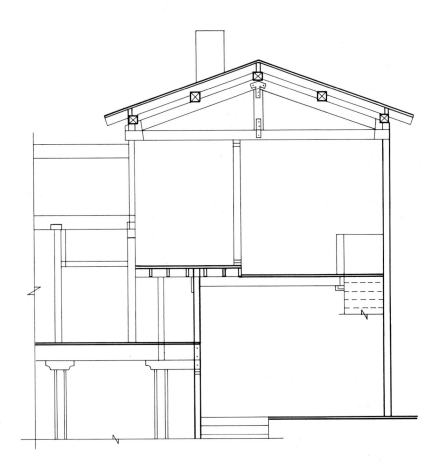

Section through tower suite

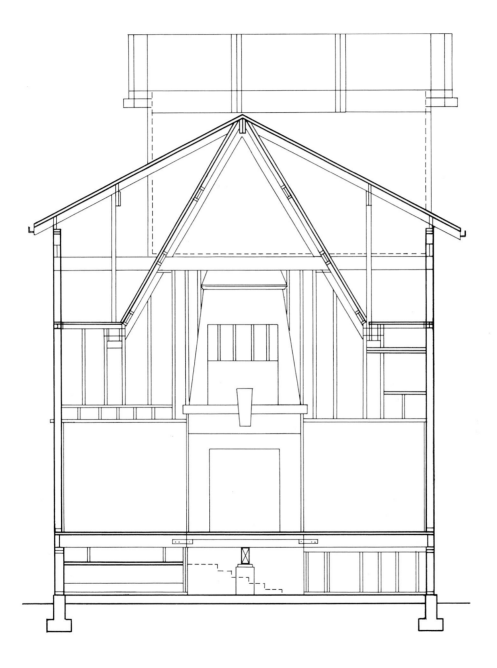

Section through the west wall of the Great Hall

Detail of staircase

Detail of Maybeck's fireplace in the Great Hall, Faculty Club

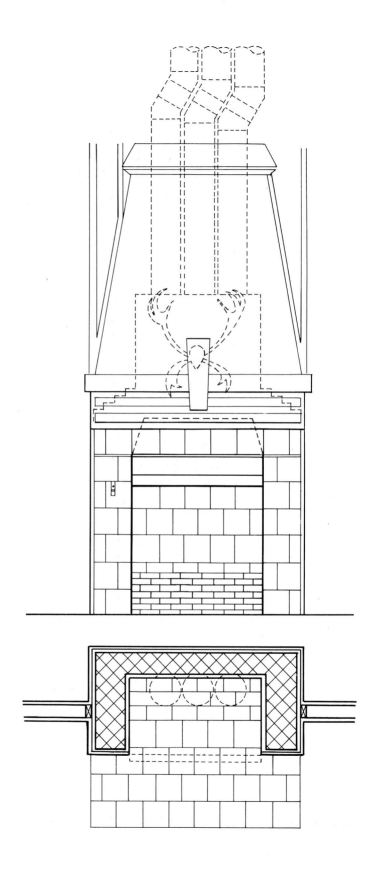

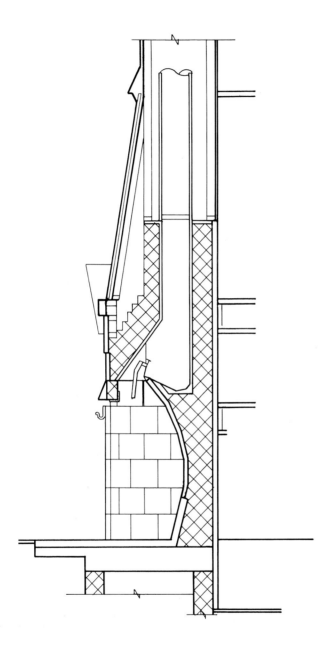

Details of fireplace in the Great Hall. OPPOSITE, FROM ABOVE: Elevation; plan; ABOVE: Section

ABOVE and OPPOSITE: Detail of the column and hammer-beams of the Great Hall

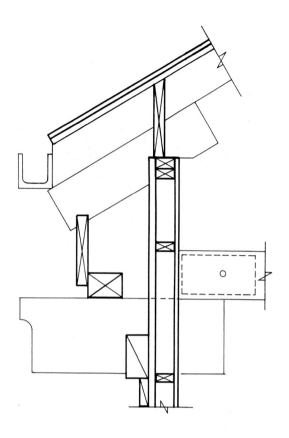

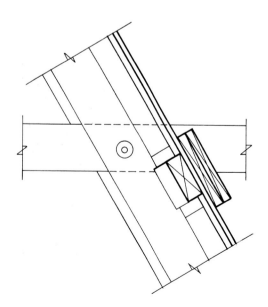

FROM ABOVE: Eaves detail; tie beam detail

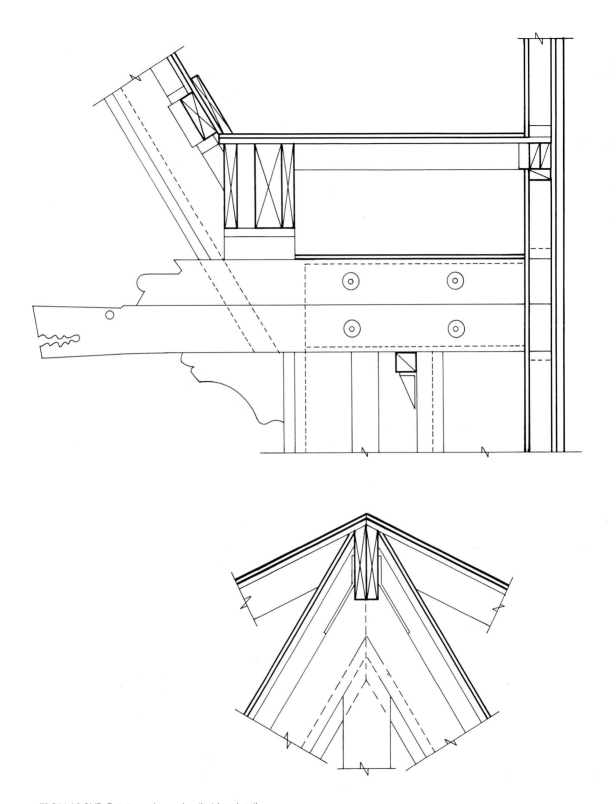

FROM ABOVE: Existing column detail; ridge detail

OPPOSITE: Detail of lamp; ABOVE: Detail of external structure

BIBLIOGRAPHY

'An Early Glimpse of the Panama–Pacific Exposition Architecturally', *Architect and Engineer*, Oct 1912, pp46–55.

Timothy J Anderson, Eudorah M Moore and Robert W Winter, (editors), *California Design, 1910,* catalogue to exhibition at Pasadena Center, Oct–Dec 1974, California Design Publications (Pasadena, California) 1974.

Herb Andree and Noel Young, *Santa Barbara Architecture from Spanish Colonial to Modern,* Capra Press (Santa Barbara, California) 1975.

Joseph A Baird, Jr, *Time's Wondrous Changes: San Francisco Architecture, 1776–1915*, California Historical Society (San Francisco) 1962.

Reyner Banham, 'The Plot Against Bernard Maybeck', *Society of Architectural Historians Journal*, no43, March 1984, p34.

Walton Bean, *California: An Interpretive History*, McGraw-Hill (New York) 1968.

'Bernard Ralph Maybeck', *American Institute of Architects Journal*, no29, Feb 1958, p68.

John Ely Burchard and Albert Bush-Brown, *The Architecture of America; A Social and Cultural History*, Little, Brown (Boston) 1961 (1st edition).

Donald Canty, 'A Highly Unlikely Maybeck Masterwork', *Architecture*, no78, 1989, pp84–9.

Kenneth H Cardwell, *Bernard Maybeck: Artisan, Architect, Artist*, Peregrine Smith (Santa Barbara, California) 1977.

Paul E Denville, 'Texture and Color at the Panama–Pacific Exposition', *Architectural Record*, no38, Nov 1915, pp562–570.

Faculty Club Minutes of the Board of Directors and other Memorabilia, University of California Archives, Bancroft Library, Berkeley.

James Marston Fitch, *American Building; the Forces that Shape it,* Houghton Mifflin Co (Boston) 1948.

Leslie Mandelson Freudenheim, and Elizabeth Sussman, *Building with Nature; Roots of the San Francisco Bay Region Tradition*, Peregrine Smith (Santa Barbara, California) 1974.

David Gebhard and Robert W Winter, *A Guide to Architecture in Los Angeles and Southern California*, Peregrine Smith (Santa Barbara, California) 1977.

David Gebhard, *Architecture in California, 1868–1968*, University of California

(Santa Barbara, California) 1968.

—, *A Guide to Architecture in San Francisco and Northern California*, Peregrine Smith (Santa Barbara, California) 1973.

Anthony Giddens, *The Consequences of Modernity*, Stanford University Press (California) 1990.

Talbot Faulkner Hamlin, *Forms and Functions of Twentieth-Century Architecture*, introduced by Leopold Arnaud, Columbia University Press (New York) 1952.

Jean Harris, 'Year's Gold Medalist, Bernard Ralph Maybeck', *AIA Journal*, no15, May 1951, pp221–223.

—, 'Bernard Ralph Maybeck, Architect, Comes into His Own', *Architectural Record*, no103, Jan 1948, pp72–79.

Henry-Russell Hitchcock, (et al), *The Rise of an American Architecture*, edited with an introduction and exhibition notes by Edgar Kaufmann, Jr, New York, published in association with the Metropolitan Museum of Art by Praeger (New York) 1970.

John Galen Howard, 'Country House Architecture on the Pacific Coast', *Architectural Record*, no40, Oct 1916, pp323–355.

Catherine Howett, 'Frank Lloyd Wright and American Residential Landscaping', *Landscape*, no26, 1982, pp33–40.

'Is There a Bay Area Style?' *Architectural Record*, no106, May 1949, pp92–97.

Stephen Jacobs, *California Contemporaries of Wright*, Princeton University (Princeton, New Jersey) 1963.

Walter C Kidney, *The Architecture of Choice: Eclecticism in America, 1880–1930*, George Braziller (New York) 1974.

Bernard Ralph Maybeck, 'Fine Arts Palace Will Outlast Present Generation', *Architect and Engineer*, Nov 1915, p53.

—, 'House of Mrs Phoebe A Hearst in Siskiyou County, California', *Architectural Review* (Boston), Jan 1904, pp64–66.

—, 'Regional Architecture', unpublished essay, file on Mills College CED Documents Collection, 1918, p6.

'Maybeck, Church, Steuben Glass Are Chosen for AIA Awards', *Architectural Record*, no109, April 1951, p11.

'Maybeck Dies at 95', *Architectural Record*, no122, Nov 1957, p24.

Ester McCoy, *Roots of California Contemporary Architecture*, catalogue of exhibition of the work of Irving Gill, Greene & Greene, Bernard Maybeck, Richard Neutra, R M Schindler and Frank Lloyd Wright, sponsored by the Los Angeles Art Commission and the Municipal Art Department, and arranged by the Architectural Panel, (Los Angeles) 1956.

Ester McCoy, *Five California Architects*, Reinhold (New York) 1960.

Philip Molten, 'Maybeck and Redwood', *Architectural Review* (London), no154, Nov 1973, pp336–337.

Louis C Mullgardt, 'The Panama–Pacific Exposition at San Francisco', *Architectural Record*, no37, March 1915, pp193–220.

Ruth Waldo Newhall, *San Francisco's Enchanted Palace*, Howell-North Books (Berkeley, California) 1967.

Official Guide of the Panama–Pacific International Exposition – 1915, Walgreen (San Francisco) 1915.

Edmund O'Neill, *An Account of the Birth and Growth of the Faculty Club of the University of California*, The Faculty Club (Berkeley) 1933.

James Gilbert Paltridge, *A History of the Faculty Club at Berkeley*, The Faculty Club (Berkeley) 1990.

Willis J Polk, 'Preservation of the Palace of Fine Arts', *Architect and Engineer*, Jan 1916, pp100–103.

'Presentation of the Institute's Gold Medal to Bernard Ralph Maybeck', *AIA Journal*, no16, July 1951, pp3–7.

Mel Scott, *The San Francisco Bay Area; a Metropolis in Perspective*, University of California Press (Berkeley, California) 1959.

Vincent Joseph Scully, *1920 – American Architecture and Urbanism*, Praeger (New York) 1969.

Harold A Small, 'The Life and Times of the Faculty Club', *California Monthly*, California Alumni Association (Berkeley) March 1966.

James C Starbuck, *Bernard Ralph Maybeck (1862–1957), The Extraordinary California Architect*, Vance Bibliographies (Monticello, Illinois) 1978.

Kevin Starr, *Americans and the California Dream, 1850–1915*, Oxford University (New York) 1973.

Ogden Tanner, 'Good Lines: Why the Houses by Bernard Maybeck are Northern California Classics', *Connoisseur*, no217, Feb 1987, pp78–83.

John E D Trask, and J Nilsen Laurvik, (editors), *Catalogue Deluxe of the Department of Fine Arts, Panama–Pacific International Exposition*, two volumes, Paul Elder (San Francisco) 1915.

Marcus Whiffen, *American Architecture since 1780: Guide to the Styles*, MIT Press (Cambridge, Massachusetts) 1969. Revised edition c1992.

Sally B Woodbridge, *Bernard Maybeck: Visionary Architect*, Abbeville Press (New York) 1992.

William L Woollett, 'Scene Painting in Architecture', *Architectural Record*, no38, Nov 1915, pp571–574.